I am
in business
with my ...

STORIES OF HOW I HELPED OVER
100 FAMILY-OWNED BUSINESSES
BECOME SUCCESSFUL IN THEIR
BUSINESSES VENTURE

Farid Ghalili

ARPress
ILLUMINATING IDEAS
EMPOWERING VOICES

ARPress
45 Dan Road Suite 5
Canton, MA 02021

Hotline: 1(888) 821-0229
Fax: 1(508) 545-7580

Ordering Information:
Quantity sales. Special discounts are available on quantity purchases by corporations, associations, and others. For details, contact the publisher at the address above.

Printed in the United States of America.

ISBN-13:   Softcover   979-8-89356-803-5
              eBook   979-8-89356-804-2

Library of Congress Control Number: 2024904013

DEDICATED TO

My Dad, Aziz – For his wisdom, his character, his generosity, his friendship, his sense of humor and above all his strong religious faith. I will always miss him.

TABLE OF CONTENTS

PREFACE

WHAT YOU NEED TO KNOW BEFORE YOU READ THIS BOOK

Every day as I leave my office to go meet with my clients for their coaching sessions, even though in most cases I have received a focus sheet telling me whether they have accomplished their tasks, and what their main challenges and their brightest achievements for the week have been, I know there is going to be a twist. A new issue is going to come up that I have to deal with and help my clients through.

In most cases, the issue arose during the week or at home, because the majority of the clients that I coach are in business with relatives. After all I am coaching owners of small to mid-sized family-owned businesses.

So, I decided to write a book about my experiences in coaching family-owned businesses and how I have been helping them. The stories are loosely based on real situations but fictionalized to illustrate certain points more clearly. I have changed the names and the business identity of the clients to protect their privacy. I am sure many business owners can and will relate to these stories.

My goal is to help business owners who are in business with family members to learn from these stories. As I tell these stories I also talk about how together we solved some of their challenges and in most cases built on their strengths.

I decided to focus this book on finances, because money is the main reason to go into a business, but secondly, because most of the issues and challenges small to mid-sized business owners face are money related. Other topics, such as team or employee issues, mixing business and family, and the rest are important. However, if the money isn't right, nothing is right. Money matters affect every other aspect of the business.

I did not want to write a textbook about the challenges of a family-owned business and how they should be handled. Many authors have written such books, which are of great value. I wanted to write about the stories surrounding these issues. I am a big fan of history. I believe we can learn from the past to shape the future. The real stories and experiences of other people can be lessons for most of us. And that is the purpose of this book.

LET US BE FORWARD

Although this book is about money matters in a family-owned business, as you read, you will begin to realize that the essence of what we're talking about is *Change*.

Throughout the book the stories, actions that were taken, the behavior of characters — their struggles as well as their accomplishments — are based on change.

In general, most of us resist change. Willingness to change, which has a lot to do with how willing we are to give up the status que and do things that are outside our comfort zone.

This book was written in the latter part of 2008, at a time when our nation as a whole felt we needed to change. Money matters and economic conditions were worse than they had been for decades at home and around the globe. The economy was a major political theme of the Presidential election. Though I have no political affiliation, I must comment that this book was written at a historic time in our country, when both parties promised to bring about change. The election of the first African-American to the highest office in the country indicates a change in the attitudes of many Americans.

As you read this book, keep in mind that the power of change is a major factor in the growth of every business — not change for the sake of change, but change for the sake of keeping up with the world. You will read about changes in using new systems, changed ways of doing things, changes in attitude, and, above all, change in our willingness to accept and work with these changes.

"There are two primary choices in life: to accept conditions as they exist or accept the responsibility for changing them." Denis Waitley.

MIXING PERSONAL BUSINESS WITH THE BUSINESS

How many times have you heard, "It is none of your business." Or "Please stay out of my business." If I had a nickel for every time, I should've asked the person who said that, "By the way what business are you in?" I would be well off.

I guess our definition of business is different. That is why I am naming this section, "Mixing personal business with the business?"

Early in my coaching career, I was coaching a couple who owned a small construction company. After two months of coaching, Susan, the wife, called me the day before a scheduled session. "Could I meet with you alone, without Jack?" Susan asked. "And — I really don't want Jack to know."

This was the first time I had received such a request, but I was to hear it many more times in my coaching years. I will be talking about them throughout this book.

I called Jack on his cell. "I just wanted to let you know that I am going to spend most of the coaching session with Susan working on financial stuff. You're welcome to sit in, but I wanted to give you the option of skipping it, if you'd prefer."

I hoped Jack would take me up on that, and he did. "That's great," he said. "I'm running behind on a project; this will give me a chance to catch up."

Jack and Susan's office was in their basement. I took my usual seat, but instead of taking out the focus sheet they'd faxed me the day before, with which I would normally start with, I told Susan, "We'll go over the focus sheet later. Let's talk about what you wanted to discuss with me alone."

You could see she was a bit uncomfortable. I reminded her, "If you recall, before we started our regular coaching session, we all promised to be open, frank and honest. Just tell me what's on your mind."

"I need to talk to you about finances and spending," she said.

No surprise there. That's an area I spend a lot of time on with all my clients.

Susan went on to say, "But first, I need to tell you something. Something you need to know if you're going to help us grow this business and teach us the things we need to know."

Her eyes teared up. She said, "Farid, you know Jack and I started this business together twelve years ago. What you don't know is that Jack and I are not really married."

Now, that was a surprise. I leaned back in my seat as she continued, "Yes this is our home; the kids you have met are ours; but Jack does not live here. We used to be married, but we've been separated for over five years, now. You need to know why, before I can actually talk about the finances and expenses."

This was obviously difficult for her. She grabbed a tissue from the box on her desk, and I tried to look calm and receptive. "You see," Susan said. "Jack started drinking and using drugs about five years ago. I didn't want anything to do with it, so we separated. Jack lives in an apartment. He comes here during the day to get the crew started, and, of course he still works here in his office." She took a deep breath. "I wish it could be different, especially for the children, but I'm okay with it."

I leaned forward, trying to be comforting. "It's okay, Susan," I said. There really didn't seem anything else to say.

"I know you're coaching us to help us grow the business and create an efficient workflow, and of course, to manage our finances. I know you can't help with the marriage situation, but you need to have the full picture."

She took a fresh tissue and said, "Now that brings me to the financial and expense issue. You have been working with me for the last three weeks to get our financial books in order. I'm starting to get a clearer picture of where we are, financially, and that's why I needed to talk to you in private."

Susan told me a lot more during that session, and I will pick her story up a bit later. But for you to understand this aspect of money management in a family-owned business, I need first to tell you what Susan meant when she said, "You have been working with me for the last three weeks to get our financial books in order."

You see most small business owners I have worked with, including Susan and Jack run their business out of a checkbook. In some cases, they do not even have a business account. They buy and pay for everything using the family checkbook!

This was not the case for Susan and Jack. They did have a business account, but they still ran everything through a checkbook and a company debit card. At the end of the month, Susan balanced the checkbook with the bank statement. If there was money in the checking account at the end of the month, they had made money; if there was no money, they had not.

Jack and Susan did fairly okay. They made money and paid their team members. Susan was considered an employee, so she got a paycheck like everybody else, but Jack used the checkbook and the debit card to cover his expenses and paid himself.

What I was working on with Susan was the conversion of all their financial records into QuickBooks files. As a matter of fact, the bookkeeper who keeps my own books also helps most of my clients get set up on QuickBooks. I have a particular way I like to set up my client's accounts so we can see the true gross profitability of the business and the profitability of each product and service they offer. At the end of this exercise, they are able to generate a Profit and Loss Statement (P&L) and a Balance Sheet which I go over with them each month. I will discuss that format later.

Once business owners move from running a business out of a checkbook, to actually having the reports needed to comprehend the business, they are transformed, raised to a new level of understanding. The financial reports, budgets, cash flow analyses, give a far more complete picture than a checkbook can. Understanding inventory management and control and return on investment of all their expenses and costs of sales makes them more effective businesspeople, with a more accurate grasp of where their business is, and where it is heading.

In many cases they actually begin to get scared. I have had clients telling me, "Farid, in one way, now that I know where my business is, I am more scared. I was happier not knowing the true picture!" Of course, later they learn how that knowledge and information can help them make decisions more objectively and run a far more successful business.

Well, Susan had learned a lot about where the money was going, and it was showing on the company's P&L. Susan continued: "Jack now lives with a woman who he met one night, I guess in a bar, and he's spending a great deal of money on her – on jewelry and other gifts, restaurants, bar tabs and God knows what else. I knew some of it," she admitted, "but the true impact on the bottom line wasn't as evident until now."

Then of course there was the subjective side. As she went on to say, "I have not bought anything new for me and the kids in a long time; we still use the same beat-up dining room table, and Jack is out there spending all this money on her!"

At this point she actually showed signs of relief. Sharing her story with someone who was helping improve the business seemed to lift a burden from her. She sat back in her chair and tried to wipe the mascara off her face. "Now you know," she said.

I told Susan, "I'm glad you shared this with me. It was very important for me to know your situation. Obviously, I don't have an answer for you right now. As a matter of fact, as your coach I do not come up with answers. I help you and Jack to come up with them." I continued, "You already know I can't help with the marriage. But we can try to make sure that what Jack is doing has the least negative impact on the company as possible. It's in both your interests to maintain the health of the company."

Now I had a challenge. I had to keep my composure, so Susan would know that I understood the problem without being shocked or overwhelmed by it. I had to think like a coach who is fully in control, as I did not want Susan to feel that this was not fixable. Inside, my thoughts started to focus on figuring out how to help these two business owners through this sticky situation.

You will read more of how I approached Jack on this issue, how we not only fixed this problem, but through business processes revitalized both the business and the marriage. Jack moved back in the house; business started to turn around; and not long after, I attended the renewal of Susan and Jack's wedding vows.

Before I share this and other stories related to money matters, let us spend some time on one fundamental element of any family-owned business. That element, which plays not just in money matters but in all aspects of the business, is *trust*.

Most people go into business with a family member because they believe that they can trust them. This seems obvious: you can trust a family member more than a non-relative. And yes, in most cases that is very true.

In the corporate world, the watchwords are, "Trust no one," "Everybody is out for him- or herself," "Watch your back." You even hear from co-workers, "I really don't trust Jim." Sometimes you do not even have to have a reason; the lack of trust is endemic in the corporate environment. In most cases, you have to live with it.

Family businesses are built on trust. The problem with that is, if that trust is broken, the impact of the break can be devastating, with far-reaching ramifications. Broken trust takes longer to restore within a family than it does in a strictly corporate environment. In some cases, it may never be restored, and the family business may even break up. It is not as if you can ask for a transfer nor have Jim fired!

So how do you solve the trust problem?

1. First, someone must admit that there is a trust problem. That person must bring the matter to the fore and create an atmosphere in which to discuss it. Not admitting that there is a problem does not work. If for the sake of not creating hard

feelings, the issue is not brought up and talked about, then progress stops.

2. If you are the person who has lost trust, be willing to restore the trust. If you take the attitude of "I will never trust him or her again, because I do not want to get hurt," then egos come into play. You must be willing to express your true feelings, but you must express them in an effective way. Hence, it is vital to learn the art of good communication.

3. You may not always agree on what caused the mistrust to start with. Everyone has their own justification so the challenge here is the art of forgiveness. If you are willing to forgive, the restoration process will be more effective.

4. Emphasize the importance of restoring trust. But the partner who has lost your trust must accept that they need to regain it. If they do not accept this, then move on, even if it means a breakup of the business. Do it gently, but do it, because without trust there is no future in the relationship, let alone in the business.

5. Restoring trust takes time, and both parties have to prove themselves. There will be a period of tests and trials. It may be, for example, that you have to audit the books for some time to make

sure you are comfortable with the outcome before letting go again.

SAVING A MARRIAGE USING A P&L

Before I tell you the next story, let me tell you how we worked out the problem with Jack and Susan.

Sometimes playing dumb can make you look smart. I called Jack the day before our coaching session and told him, "Jack in my last session with Susan working on financial management procedures, I studied your Profit and Loss Statements for the last six months. Have you had a chance to look at them yet?"

He said, "No; I didn't even know they were ready yet".

"Well, thanks to Susan they are, and I have a copy. I'd like to go over them with you and also discuss some marketing issues".

I also told him, "I've given Susan a series of action items to complete, and if we could meet alone for lunch and have our session, it would give Susan time to work on those items."

Jack said, "That would be great. Is it my turn to buy or yours?"

Laughing, I said, "Depends on if you have good news about the assignments you were supposed to work on."

I met Jack at a restaurant near their office for lunch. We spent a few minutes talking about the projects and a couple of small team issues. Then I said, "Okay, Jack, I need to explain to you some fundamentals of accounting before I actually go over your own P&L. Now remember, my intention is not to turn you into an accountant. As a matter of fact, that's not even my strong suit. But the overall concept of how I have set up your accounts, and how Susan is maintaining them, is something you need to understand first."

Jack said, "It had better be like, "Accounting for Dummies," because I've never been good with numbers".

"Me neither," I said. "Just like you, since I now own my own business, I've had to learn some fundamentals. At the same time, I've also learned how to set things up for my clients so it's easier for them to know where they stand financially."

"Farid, I've seen P&L and Balance Sheets before but frankly they are Greek to me." Like many small business owners, Jack had a problem reading, understanding and, most importantly, digesting financial information. I would have to explain to him how to read the information, what it meant, and the actions he might need to take from time to time based on this data.

Most small business owners I come across, even those that have a bookkeeper or an electronic system (software like QuickBooks or Peachtree, etc.) to maintain their financials, set up their accounts very simply. They have income accounts which may or may not even be broken into the different products or services they provide, and then they have an account of all their expenses.

So, I decided to show Jack a simple P&L and try to explain the basics.

Income	
Sale	13,500.00
Total Income	**13,500.00**
Expense	
Auto Expense	650.00
Rent	770.80
Business License & Fees	90.00
Insurance	320.00
Miscellaneous	454.45
Office Supplies	283.00
Supplies	1200.00
Payroll	7000.00
Payroll Tax Expenses	278.75
Postage and Delivery	112.00
Printing and Reproduction	19.95
Accounting Fees	80.00
Telephone and Fax	120.00
Air Fair	300.00
Meals	237.50
Total Expense	**11916.45**
Net Income	**1583.55**

I pushed our lunches to the side and showed Jack the above P&L. "Jack, of course these are not your figures. This is just to help me explain the fundamentals."

Jack did not have any problem understanding this P&L. As he commented, "With a couple of changes this could be my company's P&L."

I finished by saying, "Hopefully, if the net income is positive, you made money; if the net income is negative, you lost money."

I went on to say, "But you see Jack, as true as this may be, it does not show the real picture. Just knowing your total income and your total expenses and whether you made money or not, does not give you the real picture of the financial state of your company".

"More importantly it does not allow you to make fundamental decisions as to where to improve. It doesn't let you know if you are truly getting a good return on your investment -- on your time, your team, and the resources that goes into running your business."

Jack nodded in agreement.

I continued, "This is where I have been working with Susan for the last three weeks, to set up your accounting system so that it can help us get a better understanding of the state of your company, what products and services makes you money, and what affects your bottom line."

Jack took a deep breath and asked, "So are we making money or not?"

I said, "Yes, but before I show you your own P&L I am going to show you another one."

	Jan , 08	% of Income
Ordinary Income/Expense		
Income		
Construction Labor	9,400.00	67.63%
Material	4,000.00	28.78%
Travel	500.00	3.6%
Total Income	**13,900.00**	**100.0%**
Cost of Goods Sold		
Expense		
Auto Expense	650.00	4.68%
Rent	770.80	5.55%
Business License & Fees	90.00	0.65%
Insurance	320.00	2.3%
Miscellaneous	54.45	0.39%
Office Supplies	283.00	2.04%
Payroll Expenses		
Officer's Salary	2,500.00	17.99%
Payroll Tax Expenses	278.75	2.01%
Total Payroll Expenses	2,778.75	19.99%
Postage and Delivery	112.00	0.81%
Printing and Reproduction	19.95	0.14%
Accounting Fees	80.00	0.58%
Telephone and Fax	120.00	3.0%
Travel & Entertainment		
Air Fair	300.00	2.16%
Lodging	37.50	0.27%
Meals	200.00	1.44%
Total Travel & Entertainment	537.50	3.87%
Total Expense	**5,816.45**	**41.85%**
Net Income	**1,983.55**	**14.27%**

I went on to explain by showing Jack the next P&L example. I said, "You see Jack, an area that most business owners do not pay any attention to is the question; 'What is it cost of us to make the money we are making?' Most owners do not track their cost of Sales and Goods. Therefore, they have no idea what their true gross profit is. That is what we are going to change."

"What do you mean?" asked Jack.

I said, "When you pay your people to do a job, you need to look at each team member or even a subcontractor, to find out if they are actually making you money or not." I told Jack, "I am going to cover the concept of team efficiency in one of our coaching sessions, but just from a purely financial point of view, each team member is costing you money. So, their salary should be in your cost of sales or variable cost."

Jack still looked puzzled.

"Don't worry," I said. "I'll explain; just bear with me now".

"You see Jack, most business owners put all salaries in the expenses side in the bottom area."

Jack said, "So salaries are not expenses?"

"Some salaries are. For example, yours and Susan's are expenses. But the team and subcontractors' pay is a cost of doing business. For example, if you had a salesman on commission, his commission would be part of cost of sales, because what you pay him comes off your gross profit. The same is true of your team — what you pay them comes off your gross profit."

Jack said, "That I understand".

"Good. That's why I want you to look at each team member as someone who is either making you money or not making you money. Most of your income comes from labor, right?"

"Yes, it sure does."

I said, "Then by moving the labor cost into the cost of sales, you'll be able to tell if your labor is profitable or not".

You could see Jack was starting to get the idea.

I continued, "The same is true of the material you buy to do a job. If you can see that the price is high in relation to the income, you can decide to shop better, maybe find a vendor with better prices."

I pointed to the P&L and explained, "As you can see in this P&L, versus the one you saw earlier, here we can actually see the true gross profit. Better yet, we can see what our profit is for labor and material, in relation to the income. So when you break the income into labor income and material income, and compare it to labor cost and material cost, you can see if you are truly making money or better yet, profit, on each. We will actually do a cash flow analysis on every job you do, to make sure every job is profitable."

Jack looked at me and said, "How?"

I said, "That is what I will work with Susan on, and once she knows how to track it, I will explain it to you just as I am now. Let me ask you this," I said. "If every job you do is profitable…"

"Then the company is profitable," said Jack.

"Bingo."

I said, "Let's talk a bit about expenses, now that you can see the expenses in relationship to the income for this company.

"First you look at each item. If the expense is a high percentage of the total income, that gives you information with which to make decisions."

"Finally, you can see the net profit as a percentage of total income. That is where you can determine your return on your investment. In this particular company, the net profit is a bit over 14%, which is not bad. Our goal for your company, if you remember, is to have a 25% net income."

Jack said, "Yes, I remember. You told me for every dollar I make the company should profit 25 cents and that's after I pay myself a salary."

I smiled and said, "Yes, you're getting it. So, you are ready to see your own P&L and how hard Susan has worked to prepare it?"

Then I gave Jack a copy of his company's P&L and Balance Sheet. He took them and flipped the pages a couple of times while I sipped my coffee. Then I spent the next few minutes pointing out to Jack the numbers for his company's P&L.

I first went over the summary report, and then started going over the detail report. As I was going through the expenses, I noticed that Jack was getting curious about some of the detailed items that were showing. A couple of times he seemed to want to make a comment, but he did not.

I knew by now he had seen several of his personal expenses in the detail entry items. The report had, of course, the list of vendors and the items purchased. He seemed somewhat nervous and a bit uncomfortable, twisting the empty sugar packets into tiny knots.

For the first time, he was seeing some of his expenses on a report prepared by someone else, and that someone else was Susan. To put him at ease I said, "We won't go over every detail, but I will cover some of them from a business perspective."

I asked him, "So now that you understand the concept of gross profit, can you tell me what a business owner would do to increase his gross profit?"

He thought for minute and his first response was "Well, reducing cost will increase gross profit."

I said, "That's very true, and yes, most owners usually focus on that; but as you can see your cost, or in this case variable cost, is mainly material and labor. In a simple analysis, cutting those means either reducing labor or not buying as much material. Reducing labor could mean letting some people go, and that is not always the right option. Reducing material, unless you can get a better deal from a new supplier, would not be good either, if for example, you use lesser quality material."

"No way!" said Jack. "I pride myself on providing quality material to my customers."

I said, "Yes, I agree. So, if we cannot cut cost what else can we do to increase gross profit?"

"Increase income?"

"Bingo. That is what I wanted to hear. That is what we are going to work on, and that is a whole topic we shall cover in future sessions. But for the remaining twenty minutes we have today, I'd like to discuss some of these expenses."

I sipped my coffee. "I don't usually spend a lot of time on the expense side with my clients, as most of the expenses are fixed. In many cases, there's not a lot you can do about them. That is why they are called fixed expenses. These are items like, phone, utility, postage, etc. But looking at your report, a few items caught my eye that I normally do not see in my other clients P&L. Your total expenses in ratio to your income are very high, and as you can see your net profit percentage is low and hence the company's net profit is low."

I picked up my yellow highlighter. "Let me ask you about some of them." I highlighted several items: Meals, Entertainment, Gifts, and the ever-useful Miscellaneous. I always frown on the large Miscellaneous category.

Jack was looking very uncomfortable, especially when he noticed the names of the payees.

I said, "If you look on the right-hand side, you see the ratio of these expenses to income is very high. Can you tell me what these are? Do you entertain a lot of your customers or team members? Do you buy a lot of gifts for them?" I sat back and waited for Jack to answer.

He paused for a few seconds and said, "Are you sure these are right? Did you ask Susan if she entered them correctly?"

"Oh yes," I said. "When I saw them, they jumped out at me, and so I did ask Susan. She showed me several of the cancelled checks and credit card statements she entered these from. So, yes, I'm pretty confident that they're correct. You know Susan – she's pretty good when it comes to keeping track of expenses, sending invoices and paying vendors."

At this point Jack took a deep breath and said, "No, Farid, I do not buy gifts for my customers or any of the guys. I also do not do a lot of entertaining with them. These are all personal."

I said, "Oh, okay, you mean the gifts that you buy for Susan and the entertainment that you do when you guys go out? If that is the case, we need to handle these differently. I can explain how to handle them, so they don't affect the business." I smiled. "And so you don't get in trouble with the IRS. Those are guys you really want to stay on good terms with."

Jack seemed very tense at this point, but he didn't say anything. He was twisting sugar wrappers again.

I said, "You seemed a bit surprised at these numbers. I get this reaction from a lot of my clients. When they see the financial state of their company laid out formally on paper, it sometimes scares them."

"I guess you want me to explain these?" he asked.

I immediately responded; "Jack, I'm here to help you grow your business, make you and Susan more money, and work less. What you do with your money is not part of my coaching, but yes, the more I know, the more I can help."

"Farid, it's a long story and I know you have to get to your next appointment."

"We can leave this till our next session if you want." I said, "But I'd rather spend that time on business issues. I have a feeling what you want to talk to me about is more personal."

"Yes," said Jack. "I need to tell you something you may not know."

Well, where had I heard that before? "I'll tell you what," I said, "I'll call you tomorrow and we can schedule a lunch meeting between now and our next session. That way we can get back to our normal coaching session with Susan next week."

I told Jack "But for your assignment and goals for next week, I need you to do couple of things. One is to study this report in detail. Look at the effect of these expenses on your bottom line. Can you do that, or you need help?"

Jack rolled his eyes. "I can do it, Farid."

"Well, the second thing I want you to do is this: after you see the effect of these expenses on the bottom line, I want you to think about their wider ramifications. Think about how they affect the rest of the team, especially your main partner, Susan."

Jack shook his head. "I'll wait for your call," he said, and left looking troubled, as I flagged the waitress to bring our bill.

It was a busy week for both of us, but we found a free hour, and met at a coffee shop for the first of several conversations about his situation. I am not going to write much about that. All I can say is that eventually, Jack moved back home, and within two months after that, Susan and Jack set a date to renew their marital vows. I do not know if it was the process, or the impact of what he began to see or just that it was time. But I like to think that I played a small part in bringing about their reconciliation.

And there was a drastic change for the better in the bottom line of their company, not just from Jack's not having girlfriend expenses anymore, but from Jack and Susan's improved ability to manage their costs.

I made sure that Jack and Susan understood that they needed to separate their personal expenses from their business. Not until they took a salary or a draw from the business, could they spend it on personal expenses.

Many business owners, not just Jack and Susan, use money from their business to pay for their personal expenses, such as mortgage payments, electric bills, even clothes. I have a pretty good general idea of what can be expensed, but I usually suggest that they work with their Certified Public Accountant to understand what a business expense truly is and what is personal.

The main thing is that in a family business, mixing personal business with commercial business can have a serious adverse effect, not just on the success of the business, but on the relationship between the partners.

"For it is mutual trust, even more than mutual interest that holds human associations together. Our friends seldom profit us but they make us feel safe... Marriage is a scheme to accomplish exactly that same end." H. L. Mencken

JUST BECAUSE THEY LEND ME MONEY ARE THEY MY BUSINESS PARTNERS?

I usually do not do business coaching on Mondays but spend time working on client issues and administrative matters for my own business. One Monday afternoon, I received a call from a woman who introduced herself as Linda and asked if I had time to talk to her about coaching. "I know you're busy, and work only with selective clients, but I wanted to ask if you could help us in our business."

I always ask how someone heard about me. Linda's answer was good for the ego. "You must be very good at what you do," she said. "My husband, John, met one of your clients who bragged about how much you helped them in their business. Apparently, you improved their team morale and efficiency, and they're making more money than they ever have before."

It is always good to hear your clients brag about you. Of course, I had to know the name of the client. "Yes," I said when she told me, "They are doing very well and I enjoy working with them."

"We own an automotive high-performance shop," Linda said. "My husband is very leery about working with consultants, but after hearing all you've done for Tim and his company, he asked me to call you. I know we need help in a variety of areas, but mainly in our operations. "

Many times, when I talk to prospective clients, they feel they already know what their problem is, and in most cases, they are partly right. They do have the problem they name. However, once I start working with them, I realize that the core of the matter lies elsewhere.

I told Linda "I do select my clients carefully. It's like a coach going to a gym. Many athletes want to go to the Olympics, but the coach picks the ones he believes have promise and can be helped to achieve that goal."

Now I came to the tricky part: "And it is not only the athlete, but also the game that matters. To succeed in business, you have to be the right athlete, competing in the right game."

"What do you mean?" Linda asked.

I said, "You see, if you are a gymnast, and your goal is the gold medal you must be super good, because thousands of athletes from around the world compete in that event, and you have to beat all of them. On the other hand, if you are competing in, say, the shot put or weightlifting you need to beat only a few people to win the gold. The same thing is true in business. I look at the business as well as the owners, to determine if I can truly help them achieve their goals."

I said, "I meet business owners who have passion and a glitter in their eye about a venture in which the chance of success is not as good as they think. Imagine a man who loves to work with tools and wants to open a hardware store. He believes that because of his passion and his talent for helping people, he can be successful. So, I go with him to see the location he has picked. When we get there, he points to an empty store in a small shopping center and says that's the place for his store. Then I look across the street and see a big sign reading, 'HOME DEPOT.'"

Linda chuckled. "I hear what you are trying to say."

I said, "But then I also meet people with a business that has great potential for growth if they do things right, but after meeting with the owner I realize he's just looking for a quick fix. He's like an athlete who wants to win an Olympic medal but is not willing to come to practice and listen to the coach."

I asked Linda "So, do you and your husband believe you have the right game and are willing to work on the action items that a coach can help you with? If so, we can then take this to the next step, and I can tell you what the process is."

There was a small pause. "I know the business has potential," said Linda. "And I know for sure we need the help. But you see, the business actually belongs to my son-in-law, Larry. He's the main owner and major stockholder. We helped him financially to start this business, but he's just not running it right. So, my husband and I had to step in to help him."

Well, I thought to myself, they need the help all right, but who really needs the help? Is it Linda and John who want to protect their investment by making sure the store makes a profit, or is it their son-in-law, Larry, who needs help managing the store?

Obviously, I needed to find out a lot more to determine if I could help their business, so I told Linda "The best thing to do is to go through the process with all three of you, determine the issues and where you need help, and then go on from there."

Linda said, "That sounds great but there is some information you need to know, about why we stepped into the business and why we need help."

I said, "Okay."

"The information I'm going to share with you is just for you to know, and I'd prefer that you don't discuss it with Larry."

Where had I heard that before?

I told Linda, "The best thing is for you to send me an email. I assure you; it will be just between you and me." We went ahead and set up a tentative time to meet, subject to the availability of John and Larry.

I will cover the coaching of Linda, John and Larry soon, but after I hung up Linda's call reminded me of a couple, I had met a year or so before.

CAN A HAIR SALON MAKE IT WHEN A HUSBAND DOES NOT WANT TO CUT HAIR?

The business was a hair salon, and it actually belonged to the wife Laura. Laura and Steve, in their late 50's, had both attended one of my seminars, but Laura was the one who called to set up the appointment. I gave Laura the same talk I would later give Linda, about the type of business owners I work with. The meeting was set for an evening, after she closed the shop.

I met Laura and Steve at the salon. As I walked in, she was wrapping things up, and putting things away. Steve was under a sink, trying to fix something. There were about eight stations in the salon.

You can always tell an active hair station by the pictures, business license, scissors, combs, and hair dryer, all arranged to suit the individual stylist. As

I walked around, I could see that about half of the stations in this salon were not active.

I sat on a chair in the waiting area, and Steve and Laura came and sat on the couch opposite.

Laura asked, "Would you care for some soda or water?"

I said, "No thanks I'm okay."

I usually ask each business owner to fill out a questionnaire prior to our first meeting, so I can come prepared. I also have a comprehensive questionnaire that I use during this first session.

I start by asking a series of questions. I never say "Well, tell me about the business." I've learned that for this session such vague and open-ended questions are not effective at getting the information I need to decide if their business is a good candidate for coaching.

My first question is usually, "Tell me why you decided to go into this business."

Linda answered eagerly. "This is what I have done for years. I've worked at several different hair salons, but eventually I decided to start my own, rather than paying a portion of what I make to the salon owners."

I said, "I applaud you for wanting to own your own business."

Another question I ask is what they believe is their number one challenge. In this case, rather than asking that, I looked around and commented, "It seems as if most of your stations are inactive."

"That's one of my main issues!" Laura said. "I can't keep hair stylists! They just don't want to stay. They come, and after a couple of months — even a couple of weeks — they leave. That is where I think we need help. We can always use more clients, but there's really plenty of business, if we could only keep the hair stylists."

I was about to ask why when Steve interrupted. "You can't find good reliable help nowadays. That's the problem. We offer these women a good place to work; they make damn good money, but they're just bone lazy! Lots of times, they don't even show up to work."

I looked at Laura. She seemed to be grinding her teeth.

Steve looked at Laura and said, "Well, I'm right, aren't I? Why don't you tell him the reason they are leaving is because when we tell them they need to take this job seriously, they aren't interested.

They just pack up and go!" He looked at me and continued "Nobody wants to work hard nowadays. These women are all young and want it easy. It's not like when we worked. We had respect for the people we worked for."

At this point, even though I hate to admit it, I had in some ways lost control of my assessment session. I can't allow that when I'm there to assess the business and people. To try and take control back, I said, "Let me ask couple of questions so I can understand the issue. "

Steve jumped in again. "First, I have to tell you something: she wanted to open this business because this is what she's good at. I'm retired. I poured my entire retirement into this business, and the idea was that we would get our money back someday – that we could get the business going and sell it. Well, that's not happening. The business is barely breaking even."

I looked at Laura; she was staring at the floor as Steve continued, "We need your help to turn this business around quickly. We also need to know how to hire women who are willing to work – work! — for the money we pay them!"

He went on to say "We want to be fair, but they need to understand that this is a business. We're giving them a chance to work here, but at the end it has to be profitable for us, and for sure we need to get our investment back."

Yes, sir, I thought to myself. We do indeed have a problem here. The challenge was what my next step should be.

I said to Steve, "I agree with you, but frankly, I need to understand the core issues before I can say if I can help you. If you'll allow me, I need to ask some questions first."

Steve said, "Sure. I figured you need to do that. I just wanted you to know where I was coming from."

"Before I ask my questions," I said to Steve, "Let me ask you this. You say that you are retired." I smiled. "Looking at you in the few minutes we have chatted, I can't imagine you with scissors in your hand."

Steve laughed at the thought.

"So, tell me what you do for this business, Steve. How much time do you spend in the shop?"

Laura leaned forward in her seat and waited for Steve to answer.

Steve said, "I'm hardly here at all. I come usually when she is getting ready to close, and sometimes I help her clean up. Sometimes she asks me to come and fix a sink or the toilet or touch up paint here and there. That's all; I am mainly here to help her with whatever she wants."

"So, you are really not involved in the day-to-day operation of the business, right?"

He said, "No. But some days I do come by, and that's when I see these girls sitting around and not doing much. Frankly, I think Linda's too easy on them. Sometimes I think they take advantage of her."

I had pretty much determined the core issue here. It was not at all about marketing, customer service, operations, process control, or even team efficiency. Usually in an assessment session, once I have determined the problem, I spend an hour or so coaching the prospective client, asking about ideas they might have already tried, or I tell them what they can try, before I finally determine whether together, we can turn the business around.

In this case, even though the business could use improvements in the usual areas, there was a different problem at the core.

I turned to Laura. By now, if you could have lit her with a match, she would have exploded. "Laura what is your goal for this business?" I asked.

Steve opened his mouth.

I said, "Steve, please, I'd like to hear from Laura."

Laura said, "I love doing what I'm doing. I enjoy working on hair and training young hair stylists. If they want to work for me for as long as they want that is fine."

She paused for a second and said, "But I know that, just like me, some of them would one day want to open their own place. I really enjoy the business and I think we need help with marketing, sales, operations and team building to get this place profitable."

You couldn't keep Steve quiet long. "She needs to realize she's 55, now, and she can't do this for much longer. We need to get this business profitable and sell it."

At that point I folded my notebook and said, "I think I have a pretty good picture, and yes, you are both right. The business needs help in the areas you mentioned. If you both have the same exit strategy — to sell the business — that is what the goal should be."

Then I sat on the front of my chair, looked at both of them, and said, "But I am going to be upfront and honest with both of you. If you recall, I told you that I work with very carefully selected clients, and I am not sure I can sit here and tell you that I can truly help you achieve your goals."

Laura jerked upright on the sofa. "But I know you can! I talked with a couple of your clients after the seminar. They said how you turned their businesses around. One said you even saved their marriage! Why can't you help us?" Her eyes filled.

I hated to be in that situation. Every business owner deserves to get help, but in this case, I would not be doing them a favor by accepting them as clients.

I said, "I'll tell you what, Laura, why don't you give me couple of days and let me think about this? I may want to spend a bit more time with you and understand some issues. Then we can decide."

I stood up and shook their hands, and Laura said, "Is it okay for me to call you tomorrow?"

I said, "Please do. Even if the coaching program is not right for you, I will be glad to suggest some things that would be of help."

I drove home that evening, feeling bad in one way, knowing and I might not be able to help Laura and Steve, and good in another, because even though I had just left money on the table, I had at least not picked up a client who would not be helped by my coaching process. Steve was looking for a quick fix, and that, too, in the wrong places.

Laura called the next day. "I would like to meet you alone at the salon this evening, if you have time."

That evening, I drove to Laura's salon. She greeted me at the door, and we went to the waiting area. I took the same chair I had had the previous evening, and she sat on the couch.

After the usual polite preliminaries, Laura said. "I know you're very busy, so I am not going to take a lot of your time. You said you can't help me and my business, and I appreciate your honesty, but I know you can. I want to be sure you have all the facts before you decide."

"Steve is right; he did put up his retirement money for me to start this business, but it wasn't absolutely necessary. We have a lot more in terms of investments. It was easier for us to cash the retirement out than to sell stock. Steve has always been against my starting my own business, but he did go along with it."

I nodded as she continued "But you need to know a couple of things. One is that he comes to the shop a lot more often than he said. And none of the hair stylists that work here like him that much. He's always complaining about the business. He keeps mentioning how much money we have poured into it. They don't care about that, and why should they? They have basically rented the station and that's all. They aren't responsible for how much money we put in the place."

I could certainly understand their position.

She said, "It's *my* business, and even though most of them have their own clients, we do need to market and bring business in. But we're not doing that because we don't know how. That's one place where we need help.

"But you asked a question last night about our goals for the business. You asked something about whether we're both on the same bus. Steve told you what he wants to do, and I told you I want to keep the business."

I said, "I understand. People can have different goals."

She said, "No. You do *not* understand. We are not even going in the same direction, let alone on the same bus. As a matter of fact, if we are on the same bus, I want to get off!"

I stared at her, understanding not at all. Finally, she looked at me and said, "It's not even a matter of having similar goals. I do not want to be with him period. He does not know this, but I'm leaving him."

She added "It's not just the business that is not working. *We* are not working. I am tired of him saying, 'I poured my retirement into this business, so you have to do what I want.' He was not supposed to be an active partner in the business, the way he is. He was to support me and let me run the shop. I know he is worried about the business, but all he wants is to sell it, get his money, and cut his losses."

Whew. I took a deep breath. "Well Laura, when I take on a client, I coach the business owner. My clients have to have full autonomy in managing the business. I do have clients that have had partners raise money to start their business, but the agreements are such that they are basically a venture partner. The goal is to grow the business for the owner to eventually own it 100%." I had to give her my honest opinion. "In this case, Steve is never going to be a silent partner. Hence, the program will not work. He is looking for a quick fix, and my process is not that."

I said, "It takes four years, maybe more, for an athlete to work with a coach to make it to the Olympics and win that gold medal. I am not saying it is going to take that long for me to help a business turn around, but this is not a quick-fix program."

Laura said, "I know that, and I'm not asking for quick fix, but I also know I need some professional help."

I said, "Even though you are married, so you are entitled to some of that retirement money, he sees that as his money, that he lent to you. He considers himself an active partner, out to make sure his money is protected."

I paused, looked at her, and said, "I am sorry. If I could truly believe I could help you, I would, but

I can't take your money knowing we are not going to achieve the results we need."

By now Laura was wiping tears. I stood up, gave her a hug, and said, "Keep me posted, and call on me if there is anything I can do — any advice I can give you on marketing or bringing on the right people."

"Okay," she said.

Several weeks later I was passing by Laura's salon and noticed it was closed. The sign on the door read, "Space For Rent."

THE IN-LAWS WHO REALLY WANTED
TO HELP

Before we continue with the story of Linda and John, who financed their son-in-law's business, I must say one more thing about the case of Laura's salon. Laura and Steve's financial arrangements, being between a husband and wife, might not really have constituted borrowing money from a relative. Yet, their problems illustrate some of the ramifications of borrowing money from any relative. Every business owner needs to go into that with eyes wide open.

I am not saying you should never borrow money from family. As matter of fact, many times if it is done right, that is a better source than any other. The point of this story is that even between a husband and wife, the expectations and arrangements must be made right up front, so that it does not turn into a "Your money is my money, my money is my money, and our money is my money," situation.

And, as we will learn in the rest of this chapter, money can create other issues among family members in business.

So let us get back to Linda, John and Larry. Remember the comment Linda made: "We helped him financially to start this business, but he is not running it right and so my husband and I had to step in to help him."

I met Linda, John, and Larry at their place of business one morning at eight o'clock, two hours before they opened. We had a great session. I went through my standard assessment process and determined their general goals and objectives. I was excited about their business and its potential for growth.

They had already pretty much decided they needed to have a business coach, so most of my questions were on their willingness to work with me and, once we had defined the areas of their business that needed improvement and put together the action items, their commitment to make it happen.

We set the days and times of our regular coaching sessions so that all three could be present.

I have a very good system that I have developed throughout my years of coaching. I have a general idea of what area of the business to focus on first, second, and so on. As the business owners begin to show they have either mastered an area or are on the right track, we move on to the next area.

It is primarily the client who dictates where they need help to start with. They may not be right about where they think their most urgent problems are, but it is their business, and in theory, they should know it best. So, in most cases I give them the benefit of the doubt by asking them.

However, my experience has been that as we move through the process and I start to ask the hard questions, or as we discover an area of weakness, it often becomes evident that the real problem is somewhere else than the owner supposed. In some ways, it's not much different from going to the doctor. You think you have the flu, but the doctor discovers a different condition – a bacterial infection, perhaps.

So, in addition to their other assignments, one of the things I ask each of my clients to work on is to define, independently of one another, their top five business challenges.

Before I give them that assignment, I remind them of a talk we had during the second session about open communication and being honest and frank. I emphasize that this is something we shall practice throughout the coaching period, but if the business has more than one owner, I also assure them that if they ask me to keep certain things confidential, just between me and one of them, I will always do that.

As I had found out in my first session with Linda and John, the main business owner was actually their son-in-law, Larry. So, I spoke to him first.

"Larry, I'd like you to think about what you believe are the top five challenges that the business is facing." Then I asked the same of John and Linda. They had five days to think about that. They were to write down their thoughts and email them to me prior to our next coaching session.

We discussed other things as well. When I coach a family-owned business, an important area to discuss is the organization of the company. Like who is in charge, who is the CEO or president, CFO, etc. In many family-owned business partners feel since they have equal investment, they are both or all in charge. That creates a problem with team members because they do not know who the boss is.

I received the three emails I expected, one each from Larry, Linda, and John. I usually don't tell my clients what format to use. I want them to have the freedom to explain their thoughts in their own way. When I am coaching a single owner in most cases the list of challenges comes in bullet points.

Interestingly, in most cases when I am coaching a family-owned business with multiple owners, the lists of challenges come in the form of essays. They describe the challenges, but they also want to explain, or in many cases justify, those challenges.

These three emails were about what I expected. Larry started by pointing out that the business was doing well. It could be better, he said, but they were certainly busy. He went on to say that the lack of procedures and systems was what frustrated him the most. Everybody was constantly making mistakes, and he had to spend a great deal of his time answering simple questions. In many ways he was talking about team issues. He wrote about the fact he has not taken a vacation in a long time and had not spent much time at home with their new baby.

He paraphrased some of my comments from the previous sessions about how every business needs to have multiple marketing plans in place at all times. He mentioned that even though the business was doing well, it did not have a real marketing plan, or even marketing material. He wrote that he was really the only person who knew every aspect of the business, and therefore, he had to do all the sales work. He mentioned that the salesperson they had was really not as good as he could be.

He also had a few smaller concerns, related to inventory control, store layout and outside signs.

Since I had told them every business owner needs to have full knowledge of the financial state of his business, Larry mentioned that no one in his business really knew, month-to-month, where the business stood, financially. They did not have a system in place.

Then there was the final issue. Larry had written, "I am sure John and Linda have told you that they helped me get this business started. They have also put in some more money since then. But a few months ago, they decided I wasn't managing the business, I guess, the way they think it should be run, so they offered to come and help."

"Don't get me wrong, I can use all the help I can get. But they really don't know much about this business. And because I decided to buy a truck and a boat, which we also use as demo because we have put in high-performance parts in them, they figure I am misusing the company's funds."

He wrote "They come around to help, too, but really, they are more in the way than they are helping. Especially Linda — I can tell you; the employees are pretty frustrated with her. She's constantly questioning their work."

"We never had a formal written loan agreement, because it was all in the family, but there was never any talk about them coming and wanting to be personally involved in the business."

I was starting to get the picture, and was very curious as to what John and Linda's emails would say.

I read John's email next. John by nature was a calm and collected person. He was also a retired engineer, and very analytical by nature. He had also held some management positions in his previous corporate life. His email was short and to the point. It mentioned many things that the company lacked: formal company procedures and policy, financial reporting, team training, and a good marketing program. "Larry does need help with the business," he wrote. He mentioned that he had read Michael Gerber's book *The E-Myth* and considered Larry to be, in Gerber's terms, the technician, maybe even the manager, but not the entrepreneur.

"The business has far more potential," he wrote, "and no one is really spending time promoting it, because they do not know how." He felt the cash flow was not where it could be.

Cash flow is something I hear about from most of my clients, regardless of how the business is doing. That is when I go into my marketing coaching mode. In both my seminars and my individual coaching, I always say "I'd like to know who was it that came up with this term, 'cash flow.' It is the most ridiculous term I have ever heard. We all know that cash doesn't just flow! If it did, we'd all be standing outside with buckets! What they really mean is revenue, which is called on the P&L, "ordinary income."

I was now ready to read Linda's perception of the challenges to the business.

Linda's email did not address any fundamental challenges such as, marketing, team, process control, lack of procedures, etc. The main focus of her email was on what she saw as a lack of leadership in the company. "Larry is not a leader even though he works very hard. He can get very moody at times and it affects the whole team." She mentioned, "He is even like that at home." I was sure this was something that had been discussed between mother and daughter.

"Because he is young, he does not only not show leadership, but he engages in inappropriate conversations with employees about other employees," she wrote. "He has no concept of finances and is a big spender. He is in a great deal of debt, and we believe that he also overspends at the company's money." Then came the crux: "We have invested a lot of money in this business and in the last few months have come and helped without getting paid, and that is a problem too."

Well, I had my marching orders. I could see that coaching this business was not going to be as simple as just creating an action plan to address issues related to time, team and money.

It was going to take a certain amount of creativity to be sure that we not only made the business successful, but also did nothing that had other than a positive impact on all the people involved.

These are the types of challenges in a family business that get my adrenaline going, because I know that not only can I help them grow their business and achieve their goals, but that through the process, I can help them balance their family life, personal life and business life. As long as all the principals have the same goals and objectives, the rest of these issues can be worked out.

Larry, John, and Linda held a common vision and mission, unlike Steve and Laura who had totally different ideas as to where the business should go. However, their perception of where the problems were was different.

Through the next weeks and months, we worked together addressing all these issues. I will be writing about how we fixed the money matters in this chapter.

But I do want to talk about something that most business owners who plan on borrowing money from family members should take into consideration.

When you plan to borrow money from family members, you must realize that it is a complicated process, even though the actual borrowing may be simple as someone handing you a check. But that check comes with emotions and tension attached. The risk factors are actually far more than borrowing from a lending institution or even a private lender. Business owners who choose to borrow from family members must consider the possible repercussions.

In most cases, there are no formal agreements. Why make it formal when it is just my brother, or father, or father-in-law?

The trust that is necessary between business partners is even more necessary between borrower and lender. You trust that the person who is lending you the money is doing it to help. At the same time, the person who is lending the money assumes he or she is giving his or her money to someone he or she can trust to put it to good use.

The intentions of both parties are good, and most of the time, things work out fine. It is when they do not that the repercussions are high. If you are late with a payment, a lending institution will send you a nasty letter, but your aunt will bring it up at the Thanksgiving dinner table!

Again, as I previously stated, I am not saying you should never borrow from family members.

There are times when that is your only choice. But it should always be the last resort. And when you do plan on doing it, you should treat it as if you were borrowing from a bank and define the boundaries and rules upfront.

You should define the terms of the loan. If your family members require interest or dividends, make sure those are spelled out to both parties' satisfaction. If the family member requires shares in the company, make sure those are agreed on, and define what the value per share is. If they expect to audit the books, be prepared to show them in an agreed-upon format.

If you expect the lender not to be active in the business except for informal advice, make sure that expectation is fully defined in writing, and agreed upon by both parties. If the family member or members need something to minimize their risk factor, be prepared to discuss what, if anything, you can offer to accommodate that need.

Remember, lending institutions have ways to protect their risk. More important, if they lose because of a business failure, their loss is strictly monetary. A venture capitalist, too, lends money to a business knowing what risk he is taking. If things go bad it is purely a business matter. The only thing lost is money, and the deal is between strangers who may never do business with each other again.

On the other hand, borrowing from a family member carries the possibility of risking not only money, but the health of the relationship. Regardless of the good intentions on both sides, if things go bad, the relationship may be permanently damaged. That is the real risk in borrowing from a family member, and that is why it should be your last resort.

Larry, John and Linda obviously needed a more defined financial arrangement. There were also several other areas that needed to be addressed. For those who want to know the outcome, we did address them all. Today the business is very profitable, and everybody seems very happy.

When it came to money matters, it was very obvious, to put it harshly, that no one in that business had any clue where the money was coming from and where it was going. When they said business was good it was because they had money at the end of the month in the checking account and expenses including payroll were being met.

What was missing was financial mastery. So, we invested in a copy of QuickBooks, and I spent the next three coaching sessions going over the fundamentals of finances. Then I had my bookkeeper meet them, set up their chart of accounts, and teach them how to post their income, cost of sales, and expenses. As a matter of fact, they decided also to invest in a new point-of-sale application, integrated into QuickBooks, that was targeted at their industry.

They took a complete inventory of all the items they had bought for sale and their capital items, including the truck and the boat. Finally, they brought to date their accounts receivable (what people owed them), accounts payable (what they owed others), income, and expenses. Now they were able to generate any financial report they needed.

Having access to this information was a major eye-opener for all three of them. The loans from John and Linda were now shown on the Balance Sheet, which now gave a true picture of the company's equity.

John and Linda now had a better picture of how the business was doing. Larry began to see the impact of his way of running the business on its bottom line. He also saw what the financial status of the company really meant for John and Linda, and how sensitive he needed to be to their feelings, as well as to their investment.

We also determined that the company needed to make a lot more money than it was making. Of course, we would have to put together a comprehensive marketing plan. But most of all, the current organization had to change.

The lesson learned from this story is how financial mastery can be a major factor in a small family-owned business. At the same time consider all the factors before you decide to barrow or lend among family members.

WHO IS REALLY IN CONTROL OF THE MONEY?

M any great books have been written on managing money. I always encourage my clients to read and learn more. The purpose of this chapter is simply to share some common experiences of business owners, hoping that their experiences can help others in similar situations. I would, however, like to point out a few facts that each business owner should consider. The stories shared thus far have showed some of the ways that spending can impact a family business. We have seen, too, some of the implications of borrowing from family members.

No matter the size of the business, control over finances is absolutely fundamental. Any business owner must have a system to manage money. I have mentioned the use of QuickBooks. I do not advocate any particular money management software over other. I use QuickBooks with my clients because it is convenient for me. I use it for myself, and since my clients send me their information often to review, I suggest they use the same. It's simply easier. What I want to emphasize is that, with all the money management applications out there, there is no excuse for not using one or another of them from the very start.

If money management is outside your comfort zone, if you don't feel able to track your own financial data, there are good bookkeepers available at reasonable prices.

Make sure it is done. Tracking your financials is absolutely essential, whether you do it yourself or hire someone to do it for you.

Some small business owners are uncomfortable with financial software, and yet they do not want an employee to have access to their financials. They may try to keep track of the financials using the old-fashioned paper and pencil.

That is a big mistake, because these applications are enormously useful. Through their comprehensive reporting, they allow the business owner to see the real picture. You do not have to be an accountant or a bookkeeper to use these applications, especially with the amount of training material that is available.

I can see that the team payroll may be better kept confidential, and you can always outsource that. But I encourage my clients to share with their team their company's financial goals, as well as the weekly, monthly, quarterly, and annual actual and budgeted figures for sales and cost of sales. They are part of your team, and it is as much their responsibility as yours to help achieve those goals.

I have had owners who don't like the idea of team members' knowing what the business makes. They fear that the response will be, "Oh, sure, I work my tail off so he can get rich."

This information sharing is one of the most misunderstood concepts in owning a small or mid-sized business. But part of growing a private business is to think like an owner or shareholder of a publicly held business.

Many of my clients were amazed when they started sharing their financial numbers, with team members. Often, they are amazed how often team members have come forward with ideas on how to create efficiency, cut costs, and even increase revenue.

Regardless of who does the books, business owners must be in control of the financials and always be fully aware of the financial state of the company.

DELEGATION VS. ABDICATION

I had started coaching Dave, the young owner of a construction company. His expertise was, of course, in design, and he was very good at it. He had a large crew, with a couple of superintendents and four foremen. I met him when he and his office manager, Margaret, attended one of my seminars.

After the seminar, I noticed that they both waited behind to talk to me. Margaret, who looked to be in her sixties, dragged Dave, much younger, to meet me after most other people had left.

As Margaret and Dave approached, I greeted them, shaking their hands and saying, "I hope you enjoyed the seminar and learned some things you can implement in your business."

"Sir —" said Margaret.

"'Farid' will do."

"Okay, Farid. After listening to everything you had to say, I realized we aren't doing any of the things you talked about."

I said, "Not surprising. That's usually the case."

"I work for Dave, here. He owns a design and construction company."

I looked at Dave and said, "Great! How's business?"

"We are actually doing really good." said Dave. "Business is great."

"Wonderful," I said. So, what did you take away from the seminar tonight?"

Before Dave could answer, Margaret said, "We're not making any money".

I felt a bit puzzled and couldn't help smiling." I hope you're not doing this for free?"

Dave smiled too, and said, "What she means is that the profits aren't what they need to be." He gave me a sheepish look. "You talked a lot about the difference between revenue and profit. Our revenue is high, but our profit is basically nothing."

I sometimes, if the timing is right, ask about their revenue and profit. So, I asked "If you don't mind telling me, what was your revenue last year?"

Dave hesitated, but said, "Somewhere in the neighborhood of six million."

"Good, very good for a mid-sized company."

Margaret looked impatient. "Tell him how much you took home, Dave."

I looked at Margaret and said, "You mean his salary, or the company profit?"

Margaret said, "I do the accounting and the payroll, and I can tell you he doesn't take any salary." She shrugged. "And if you add up all that he took home over the past year, it came to less than $80,000 — just about $76,000."

I blinked. "You did over $6 million in revenue and took home only $76,000?"

"I guess," Dave said. "She's probably right; she knows my company numbers better than anybody."

Ah. That was the first problem. I said to Dave, "I don't know much about your company, operation and finances but something isn't right."

"I've been with him since he started the business eight years ago," said Margaret, "and he doesn't listen to me, but we need help. What he needs is a coach".

At this point, considering their relative ages and her anxiety for and genuine interest in Dave, I assumed that Margaret was Dave's mother.

I looked at Dave and said, "Well, if that is what you need, we can set a time to talk, do an assessment of your business and go from there."

Dave looked hopeful. "Like she said, we're not doing most of what you talked about, and if you can help us – hey, that would be great!"

The next day, I called Dave to give him my standard talk and set up a time to meet. I said, "I usually meet with both the business owners, so would that be you and Margaret?"

Dave said, "No Margaret is my office manager."

I said, "Oh, it's not often I see office managers wanting to hire a business coach for their boss. She must care a lot about you and the business."

Dave said, "Well she has been with us for a long time."

I met Dave at his office on the day he had setup for his assessment. The meeting went fine and we both decided that the coaching program would help him and his company not just for profit but several other areas we talked about.

After the assessment process, Dave took me around the company and introduced me to everyone in the office as his new business coach. In one of the corner offices there was an attractive lady sitting behind a desk. Next to her desk was a baby dressed in pink, in a crib.

Dave said, "This is Fay and she is my boss." He then turned to Fay and said "Well, this is Farid; he is now my new business coach."

Fay stood up and shook my hand and said, "I have heard a lot about you. Dave has been looking forward to this meeting, and was anxious you would consider being his coach, but as his wife, I must tell you that you have your work cut out for you."

I hadn't realized Dave's wife worked there. Of course, if I had known, I would have made sure she was included in the assessment process. The questionnaire that Dave had filled out asked if there were other decision makers in the company, and he had answered No.

"Who is this gorgeous one?" I asked, walking towards the crib.

Fay said, "This is our daughter, Megan."

"Thank God she takes after her mom," I said, smiling.

"That's for sure," said Dave.

"So, Fay what you do here besides being the boss?"

Fay laughed. "I'm only part-time. I help Dave with some of his CAD work."

You will read more about Fay later. But before I discuss the money matters related to this business owner, I must tell you about an incident that shed a great deal of light on some of the fundamental issues Dave was facing.

Most of my clients pay for my services by electronic funds transfer. One reason for that is that it is simpler. Another is that I usually do not like to have money issues between me and my clients during our coaching sessions. My relationship with my clients is that of mentor, confidant, and friend. Therefore, I try to keep my fees out of it.

During my assessment session I explained my reasoning, and set this up with each client. Usually there is no problem with this at all. Dave did not have any issue with this either, when I asked him to fill out the EFT form. However, the next day, he called me and said, "Margaret has a problem with paying you via EFT. She said something about people having access to our bank account. I'm really not sure. It's no big deal — just work it out with Margaret when you come the next time".

The next time I came for Dave's coaching session, Margaret waylaid me as I walked in. "Look, Farid I don't like doing automatic payments – is it okay if I send you a check every month?"

I said, "That's not how I usually operate, Margaret. I've explained it to Dave, and he's okay with it. What seems to be the problem?"

Margaret twisted her hands together. "That would really screw me up, Farid. I wouldn't have control over all the bank withdrawals anymore. I'd really rather not do it. Everyone else has always been willing to take checks."

Well, I thought, this is going to be one of the areas that Dave and I have to work on anyway. No point in making an issue of it now. I said, "Margaret for now that is okay. We can do it your way, but I would like to discuss this with you at a later time".

Three coaching sessions had passed, and one day as I was leaving, Margaret called me into her office and said, "Farid, I was going to mail your check today but since you are here, I'll just give it to you." She smiled "That will save us the postage."

"No problem," I said.

She turned to her computer. "Oh I need to bring up your company name".

I started to walk around her desk and look at the terminal, but she said, "Oh please stay on that side. I don't let anybody watch me while I'm working, especially when I'm paying bills."

I stepped back and said, "Sorry."

She looked up at me. "I'm very cautious about who has access to my computer."

I said, "It sounds like it."

She said proudly," No one can access this computer not even Dave. I manage our accounts very tightly and make sure everything is done right".

Suddenly a whole new set of issues went through my mind. I repeated her words in my mind "No one – not even Dave". I knew that sooner rather than later, I had to start the coaching sessions related to finances and money.

While driving to my next appointment, I thought about Margaret. She had no idea that once we started getting into financial controls, Dave was going to be intimately involved. Even the way they manage their books and reporting was going to change. Margaret was going to go through the roof.

True, it was Margaret who had insisted that Dave needed a coach. It was Margaret who was worried about Dave's not making any profit. But then, it was Margaret who was in the way of Dave's fully understanding his business problems.

Margaret was going to be a challenge.

Two sessions later, I told Dave "Okay — today we start discussing financial issues".

Dave asked if Margaret should be part of the session, since she took care of the financial issues.

"I'm sure at some point, when we get into action items and what has to change, she will be involved," I said. "This session is only to cover fundamentals."

So far, Dave and I had been working together for about four weeks, and Dave impressed me as being overwhelmed. During each session he would bring up several challenges that he was facing with the crew. He would talk about many mistakes that were being made in the field. He always got calls during our session, even though he never answered them.

One of his biggest challenges was managing his time. Dave and I covered some time management issues. Those were the areas that we had been working on for the past four weeks. Even though we had a long way to go on those matters, I needed to start talking about finances soon.

I asked Dave "Do you by any chance have copy of a recent P&L?" He said, "I don't, but I am sure Margaret will have it." He called Margaret and asked, "Do we have a recent copy of our P&L?"

Margaret said, "No, Pete keeps those."

" Who is Pete?" I asked.

Dave said, "He is our CPA."

I said, "Well, yes, I'm sure he does have a copy — but isn't there a copy here?"

"I guess not," said Dave. "I can have a copy for you next time."

"Dave, when was the last time you looked at your P&L and Balance Sheet?"

Dave thought for a bit and said, "I don't know. I guess it's been a while".

I said, "Dave let me ask you again — when was the last time you looked at your P&L?"

You could see Dave was getting a bit uncomfortable. He said, "Honestly, I don't remember."

I said to Dave, "Do you see the picture I see here?"

"What do you see?"

"I see a business owner who owns a company that does over 6 million dollars in revenue. He employs close to forty people. Someone else manages his money. He works ten to twelve hours day — and takes home less money than several of his employees."

Dave took a deep breath.

I said, "Something wrong with this picture?"

Dave nodded. "Yes."

I said, "So, do you agree that we have to repaint this picture?"

Dave said, "Yes, and what you're telling me is that *I* have to repaint it."

I said, "Yes. But the good news is, I will show you how."

Dave said, "Well, that's why I hired you."

"Well, Dave no," I said. "Even though you pay me, I don't work for you. You aren't my boss, and I'm not yours, either. I am your coach, and I am here to help you achieve your goals."

I said "Seriously, I am going to ask you to do things that are outside your comfort zone. I know you enjoy the design part of the business, but you are going to learn how to take back control of the other aspects of the business, also. I'll ask you the question I asked everyone in my seminar: Do you want to be a business owner, or do you only want to be self-employed?"

Dave smiled and said, "So when do we start painting?"

I smiled back and said, "Well, speaking to an engineer: you understand better than anybody that first we need to redraw the new picture, and then we can paint it."

I said, "Dave, I'm going to spend the next two to three weeks teaching you the fundamentals of understanding your financials. Next time we meet, I want you to bring your Balance Sheet and copies of your P&Ls for the last six months. You don't have to be an accountant, but we do have to make sure you can read and understand those reports".

I took a deep breath and gave him the bad news. "I warn you; you may see information in these reports that you're not happy with. Especially once you understand them! But it's all part of the process of redrawing the picture."

Dave looked solemn.

I said, "Also, we're going to make some fundamental changes. Some changes Margaret is not going to like. You need to be ready for that."

Dave brushed that off. "She'll be fine, Farid! She's very loyal. Remember, Margaret is the reason you are here."

I thought to myself, "He has no idea." I agreed by saying "I'm sure she is, but my experience is that people, especially those who are set in their ways, have a hard time with change. And this process we are going through is all about change."

On the way out I stopped by Margaret's desk. This time, I didn't try to go around and look at her computer screen!

I said, "Margaret, Dave is going to have Pete send copies of his last Balance Sheet and the last six months' P&Ls. But I'd like to talk to Pete before

I come next time. Can you give me his contact information?"

You could see she was full of questions. She said, "Sure, but just so you know, he's really retired; he only does few accounts. He's actually my brother-in-law," she added. "He doesn't charge us a lot and does our books and files our quarterly and end-of-year taxes."

I took the paper she handed me. "Thanks. I just want to introduce myself. He's going to be part of some of the changes we'll be making in how we report things."

"Like what?" she asked anxiously.

"I'll go over all that with you and Dave," I said." Remember, the secret to why Dave's taking home only $76,000 is in those reports."

I called Pete the next day. I introduced myself as Dave's new business coach.

At first, he had no idea what I was talking about. So, I went into my 60-second elevator speech, about what I did working with small to mid-sized businesses and helping them grow.

When he seemed to get it, I explained that I was going to spend some time with Dave, helping him understand his P&L and Balance Sheet.

Silence for a couple of seconds on the other end of the phone. Then Pete said, "Good luck."

"You don't sound very confident."

Pete said, "What was your name again?"

I said, "Farid. But spelled with an "i," not a double "e"."

Pete said, "Faheed, I've been trying for years to get Dave to look at his P&L and let me show him where some of his problems are. I hope you have better luck than I did."

I said, "Well, I'm helping him with every aspect of his business, but as you know, at the end of the day, nothing's much good if he's not making money."

"You can say that again," said Pete. He hesitated for a moment. "I'm sure you've met Margaret. She takes care of his books and manages his accounts. She's actually pretty good. With Dave being young and not knowing much about business, he's lucky to have her."

I said, "Yes, she seems to care about him."

Pete said, "She is family." He laughed. "Literally, in my case. She's, my sister-in-law. I don't know if she told you I'm retired. I only keep books for half a dozen of my old clients."

I said, "Yes, so she said. She thinks very highly of you. Look, I've asked Margaret to get a copy of their last six months P&Ls and their last Balance Sheet from you."

"They're all here," Pete said. "You can have them any time." He sighed. "I'm glad somebody is going to help that young man. He's a good engineer, but when it comes to managing his money, he has no clue."

I said, "Well, that's about to change."

"So," asked Pete, "Are you going to manage his books?"

I blinked. "No! Oh, no. I'm going to teach him how to use the information himself. As a matter of fact," I added, "I will need your help in making some changes to his chart of accounts. I want to break it up, so I can help him understand where he is making money and where he is not."

"Glad to help." said Pete. "But like I said I am just doing this for a few people. I'm almost 75; soon they may have to find someone else to take over."

I said, "Pete, just stay with us for while, will you?"

He laughed. "Oh, I can probably manage a few more months. I sure am glad Dave's getting help."

My client's CPA's and accountants are usually very helpful during this process. Sometimes I find one or two who are hesitant in making the necessary changes. In most cases, the hesitant ones are simply set in their ways. They try energetically to explain that the new way is not good accounting, that they have been doing things their way for a long time, and so on.

Usually, though, I have no problem convincing them that it makes sense to look at things from a business point of view rather than purely from an accounting point of view.

It was delightful to talk to someone like Pete, who was so open to working with us. During the whole process, he was very helpful. He even — eventually — learned how to pronounce my name!

During our next session, I explained to Dave how to read and understand P&Ls and Balance Sheets. We went over his P&L and Balance Sheet, and I explained the difference between his, and the ones I was proposing.

Their chart of accounts, like that of most companies, showed only one item under income: "Sales".

I pointed out that we needed to break the income down, attributing it to the different services they offered.

I suggested we also break the income down according to different target markets. For example, he should show income from commercial sources vs. from government vs. from other institutions.

Then of course, the cost of goods were to change to show labor and materials for each of the various income categories. We would also modify several of the expense items.

Once Dave understood why we needed to make the changes, he was delighted that soon he would be able to figure out where his business problems lay.

I used the same examples that I had used with Jack. The only difference was that in Jack's situation, Susan was the one I worked with, since she was a partner and basically the CFO of the company. Therefore, she had a great incentive to create the financial system we were proposing.

In this case I needed to get a buy-in from Dave first. Once he understood the issues, we could begin to work with Margaret and Pete to make the necessary changes.

Of course, Pete wasn't the main problem. What was going to be a problem was the changes Margaret would have to adapt to. Pete had warned me that Margaret was not going to be happy with any changes that would impact on how she had to operate.

You see when you implement this type of system it creates discipline in most businesses. It creates a great tool for the owner, who begins to see a true picture of the business. But the discipline it creates is outside the comfort zone of many — office managers as well as business owners.

This is where a small to mid-sized business owner has to step up to operate like a big business. Accurate records are key to successful growth.

Dave was on board. Pete was on board. So far this was the good news.

The bad news was that Pete was using a very old accounting application. He'd been using it for years. To do the books for a few companies in his retirement, he'd never needed to upgrade.

Margaret, on the other hand, was using Peachtree for creating invoices, and paying vendors. They actually used an outside service for payroll.

Every month, she would send Pete a set of reports, and he would enter all the data manually and create the P&L and Balance Sheet, which, actually, no one ever looked at. Margaret also wrote the checks for the quarterly taxes.

Pete was ready to make the changes in the accounts, even in his old system. The challenge was to get Margaret to change her old accounts to match the new accounts, which would keep track of things in a lot more detail than she had been used to.

I told Dave, "Talking to Pete, he sounds ready to make these changes I've been very pleased with his cooperation."

Dave said, "He called me. You should have heard him! He kept saying, 'I've been telling you for years that you need to make some changes! What, does it take a coach to make you do it?'"

We both laughed as I said, "This is all part of that repainting." Then I paused and said, "But you know we are going to have a problem with all of this, don't you?"

"What problem?"

"According to Pete, his sister-in-law is not going to be happy with all these changes."

It took Dave a couple of seconds to figure out what I was talking about. He grinned. "Oh, you mean my self-proclaimed Mom? Margaret has always been a trouper; she'll be fine. I'm not worried about her."

I said, "Dave she is trouper, but I can assure you she will put up a fight like a commando. Trust me, I know."

Dave said, "Why are you so concerned about her not wanting to do this?"

I had to educate Dave, because if we did not do this transition correctly, one of three things might happen. The process might fail. Margaret might quit. Or, worst of all, no change would occur in their financial system. That would defeat my whole purpose in being there.

I said, "Dave let me ask you couple of things and it will become clearer."

I could see that Dave was now getting anxious. Just like most business owners he had no idea what I was trying to tell him.

I said, "Dave, first answer this question: Is there anyone here who can actually pay the bills, send out invoices, pay the taxes, and send information to Pete, other than Margaret?"

Dave thought for a bit and said, "I guess not." He raised a finger. "But she always does that, even when she's sick or has to take time off. She always makes sure it gets done."

I sat back and gave Dave time to think. I could almost see the gears meshing in his mind.

"Farid, I never even thought about it. I never had to worry about it."

"My point exactly. When was the last time you actually got on her system and tried to get any information?"

He said, "I never have. I always ask her for it."

I said, "Dave you couldn't access the information even if you wanted to. Her computer and all the information in it might as well be in Fort Knox. No one can access it except her. Did you know that?"

His look said he hadn't known.

I said, "Dave, you're not knowing is a problem by itself that we'll need to address at some point. But the point I am trying to make right now is about control. Control is the reason it's going to be difficult to make the financial reporting changes you need. Margaret will lose control of a lot of information that she has had that no one else has had. And second, she is going to have to do things very differently than she does now."

I looked at Dave and said, "Once you and your management team become aware of these financial data, you'll begin to ask questions. You'll want to have the information you need to run an effective, profitable operation. You and the team will ask questions that up to this point, only Margaret has had the answers to."

I said, "Dave I'm not going to use the standard cliché of what happens if, God forbid, she gets hit by a bus. But are you getting what I am trying to tell you?"

Dave fiddled nervously with a pencil. His face looked troubled. For the first time someone had spoken aloud the questions that I am sure had gone through his mind, but that he'd never had to answer.

To ease his anxiety I said, "We'll have to come up with a strategy to work this problem out. The good news is, I can help you through it. But we are not going to solve this today." I continued, "So, here's what I'd like you to do for our next session: I'd like you to think of ways that we can address these issues with Margaret and make this transition smooth."

I paused and said, "Margaret cares a lot about you, and that level of loyalty is something I don't see in a lot of my other clients' team members. So, at the end, if we do it right, I'm confident it will work out. You know her better than I do. So, think of ways we can help her with this transition."

I said, "I will work with her on the tactical issues, so the transition and the changes she has to make are easy. I also know she trusts Pete, and he can help. But as I said, it's not the changes themselves, as much as her loss of control. She's going to have to open the lock to the information that she feels is hers alone."

Dave took a deep breath and thought for a few seconds and said, "That paint job is not going to be easy, is it?"

I smiled back and said, "Trust me; you'll will be painting pretty soon, but we need to work on the drawing, and maybe even put some primer on first."

I stood up, shook his hand and said, "See you next week. Make sure you send me your focus sheet."

He said, "Oh, yeah. Sounds like I have a few things to focus on."

The next day I found a voice mail from Fay, Dave's wife. I called her back while driving to a session, she said, "Do you have few minuets to talk now? I'm at home and Megan's down for her nap."

"Sure. What's up?"

"Dave told me you and he had quite a conversation about Margaret."

I said, "Yes, I think it was an enlightening session for Dave."

"I can imagine," Fay said. "You know, Dave and I met and got married years after he started the company. So, most of his people, including

Margaret, have been with him longer than we have been married."

I said, "Okay."

"I'm usually not involved in the business much. I just help him with some of his engineering drawings, using the CAD system in the office. Actually, that is how we met — he was taking a CAD class".

"Cool," I said. "But about Margaret."

"Yes, sorry. I've been telling him and *telling* him all the stuff you told him yesterday. I've seen it, working in the office. Everybody tiptoes around her."

Then she seemed to backtrack hastily. She added "Of course, she's very loyal to Dave and very good at what she does."

I said, "I know that." "But she thinks she is, like, next in charge. Sometimes it even feels like she *is* the one in charge! Dave has given her a lot of authority, a lot of control. She gets bossy sometimes, even with the superintendents and the foremen." Fay sighed. "I'm tattling on Margaret, and I really care for her because of her loyalty to Dave."

I said, "Fay, I know. Trust me. I need to know these so I can help." She said, "After Dave told me about your conversation, I was so excited that at last someone had confronted Dave with this issue. Knowing Dave, I think for the first time yesterday, he actually realized he may have a problem that he needs to fix."

I said, "That was the idea. And I am sure he will fix it. We just need to do it in the right way to make sure everyone comes out of this feeling good, and we do what is best for the company and for you, Dave and Megan."

Fay said, "Thank you and if there is anything I can do please let me know." I said, "Fay thanks for calling me and in future if you see things I need to know pleas let me know."

She said, "Also keep your promise to Dave that soon he is not going to be working as many hours as he has been." I said, "That is the main goal." Fay said "Bye" and I continued to drive.

WHO DECIDES WHAT GETS PAID?

One of key challenges that is very common among small to mid-sized businesses, is that the business owner spends hours dealing with billing, collections, paying bills, managing credit cards, and all the verbal and written communication associated with the business.

This kind of work is a time sink that can result in the owner's being so occupied working *in* the business, that he or she has no time left to work *on* the business.

If you have multiple owners, like Jack and Susan, it becomes a bit easier. Susan, you remember, oversaw financial matters in their business.

On the other hand, when you leave these tasks to an office manager or bookkeeper who is a salaried or hourly team member, you need to set up rules, boundaries, and controls. Otherwise, you will end up in the situation that Dave was now in with Margaret.

In most cases I have found that in business, just as in any game, you have a greater chance of winning if the rules of the game are defined, and if plans B and C are in place before the game starts. If things do not go the way they should or untoward circumstances occur, like a player getting injured, then as the owner, you can call the next play.

We had a situation here where Dave because of several reasons, had abdicated his responsibility for the financial state of his company. He thought he had delegated it, but there is a distinct difference between delegation and abdication.

This happens to many business owners. Here are some of the reasons:

- They are very busy working in the business.
- Financials and numbers are outside their comfort zone.
- They believe they have a person they can fully trust to manage all of that, so they do not have to worry about it.
- All of the above

In many cases, business owners trust a team member so much that they even give that person signature authority. If not done right, this can be very dangerous. I must admit that Dave had not actually given Margaret check-signing authority. However, many a time while I was there, she would come in and would ask Dave to sign one or several checks, and he would not even question them. "I need to take care of these today before you leave," she would say, and he would sign. This was as bad as if Margaret had been signing the checks herself.

You can indeed create a system in which things flow smoothly, without the risk either of losing control or of getting bogged down in financial detail work.

I received Dave's focus sheet a day before our next coaching session. In the area of his learning, he indicated that he now understood how vulnerable his company's financial arrangements were, and hence to a great degree, how vulnerable his entire operation was, and why he needed to do something about it soon.

I noticed in his comment section he did not have a proposal except to say, "Work with Farid to create an action plan."

But in his goals section, though he gave no details, he did indicate that he needed to have a backup plan for Margaret's work.

I called Dave on his cell as I knew he might be out in the field. When he answered I said, "I got your focus sheet. Have you given any thoughts as to how we are going to deal with the issue?"

Over the noise of construction, he said, "I have. I know what we have to do, but frankly I am not sure how."

I said, "Okay, I am going to spend the first twenty minutes of our next session explaining to you how we are going to approach this. Then, for the rest of the session, we need to have Margaret, and even Pete, if possible, come in and join us."

I hung up knowing I had couple of days to come up with a plan.

On our coaching day, as I passed Margaret's office, I noticed an elderly gentleman sitting with her. When I walked in, he got up and held out his hand. "I guess you're Farid?"

I said with a smile "I bet they call you Pete".

He said, "Yes, it's good to put a face to a name."

Margaret said, "I guess we are all meeting today?"

"I hope so," I said. I'm going to spend few minutes with Dave, and then we can all regroup."

"I reserved the conference room," she said.

I said "Oh, that actually works great. I may need to use the whiteboard".

Dave was in his office, on the phone. When he hung up, and looked at me and said, "Pete's here."

"Yes, I just met him in Margaret's office."

He leaned back in his chair and said, "So what's the plan?"

I grinned at him and said, "Hey, I thought that was what you were going to work on. I noticed on your focus sheet you put the job on my back."

He opened his mouth to say something, but I forestalled him. "I do have a plan, Dave. Let me tell you what I am proposing, and then you tell me if you think it will work."

He said, "I'm all ears."

"You see, Dave, this must be Margaret's plan. Not mine, not yours but actually hers."

Dave seemed a bit puzzled, so I said, "Let me explain."

If a person is an alcoholic and you are trying to help them, what is the first thing that has to happen?"

Dave said, "They have to admit they are one and agree to get help."

I said, "Good. And you know that is an addiction that they have to break."

I moved on "If a person is a smoker and enjoys it and has built a habit, but deep inside knows that long term it may even kill them, and there are people who want to help that person — what has to happen first?"

Dave said, "He has to want to quit, and be willing to accept help."

I said, "One last example. You have a person who loves to drive fast and is always going miles over the speed limit. And he knows that he may one day get pulled over but continues to do it."

Dave smiled and said, "Have you been following me?"

I laughed and said, "No, but if you have not gotten any tickets thus far, one day you will. But seriously, if it has happened to you, you know. What happens when that person gets pulled over one day and as matter of fact the speed is so high that he must go to court rather than just pay the fine."

Dave said, "He is not going to be happy. As a matter of fact, it happened to me. I don't drive that fast anymore, especially with Fay and Megan in the car." He looked quizzically at me. "All right, all right, I get it, Farid."

I said, "I know you do. What Margaret has to do, is to recognize and face the problem on her own. That's why this must be her plan."

I said, "We are going to spend the time to bring out the consequences of how things are. The current status. Then we'll show Margaret how things can be. Better ways of doing things that would make her life easier. Then I promise you, with your help, she will come up with a plan."

I told Dave "You see it is all about getting outside that comfort zone. And it is all about being in control. Once you realize the ramifications and at the same time see the benefits, you will want to make the change."

Dave said, "Well, I know she doesn't smoke, and she doesn't drink, and she drives like a snail."

I laughed and said, "Trust me, after our chat with her, she will feel she does all of those."

Dave said, "I'd sure like to see how you're going to do this."

I said, "Not me. We. You just follow my cues."

Dave, Margaret, Pete, and I sat down at one end of the table in the comfortable conference room. Coffee, tea, and a dry-erase board: perfect.

I started by saying "Well, today we are going to cover a good portion of financial reporting. We are not going to implement a lot of changes, but mainly talk about some of the changes that we'll need to address in the next few weeks."

I turned to Pete and said, "Pete, I really appreciate you taking time to help us through this process."

"Yeah, Pete," said Dave. "Thanks for coming on such short notice."

Pete said, "No problem — anything I can do to help."

"Before we really get into the main topic," I said, "I'd like to spend few minutes bringing you up to speed about these coaching sessions. Before I begin to engage the rest of the team, I work with the business owner, going over some key issues and the fundamentals of a business. This gives me a chance to understand the areas that we need to home in on."

"Dave and I also been talking about where he should be spending his time, and how he should begin to create a weekly default calendar to follow."

Margaret looked at Dave and with a big grin said, "You, following a calendar? This I have to see to believe."

I sat back in my chair and looked at Margaret. "Margaret if he does and we all implement some of the changes we're going to make, he has you to thanks for, right?"

Margaret looked a bit proud and said, "I guess. I knew it would take someone from outside to help him run this outfit better."

The stage was set. My goal was to engage Margaret in this whole process, to prepare for the areas where she would be the one operating outside her comfort zone.

I asked her, "That night at the seminar, when we talked, what was the primary reason you waited to talk to me afterwards?"

She thought for a bit and said, "Well, the fact he is not making as much money as he should."

"Right. At the same time, do you remember the topics I covered in the seminar? It wasn't all about money, even though at the end everything I talked about would affect a company's bottom line. In fact, if I recall, your own words were, 'We are not doing *any* of the things you talked about.'"

She nodded. "Yes, I remember."

I glanced over at Pete. "Pete tells me he's more than ready to fully retire and turn over the accounts he's working on to someone else."

"Yes," Margaret agreed. "He's been saying that for awhile."

I looked at Pete and asked "Well, Pete if you had your choice, when would you want to do that?"

Pete put his pen down and said, "Actually, I wanted to do it a couple of years ago. But have not. I wanted to make sure all my clients found someone to do their books first. But Dorothy is insisting that this had better be my last year."

"My sister," Margaret explained.

"We really need to go and spend some time with the grandkids," Pete said. He sounded a bit wistful, I thought.

I said, "Yes, these times are too precious times to lose. Grandkids grow up."

"And he has eleven of them," Margaret pointed out.

I grinned and said, "Well, a month with each and that covers the whole year, almost."

Pete turned to Dave. "Seriously if we can find a good accountant for you, I'd like to start doing that."

Dave said, "Pete you've been doing a great job for us all these years, but you're entitled to retire. If you and Margaret can find us a good accountant, we can start the transition any time."

I looked over at Margaret. Though she was silent, I could see a lot going through her mind.

Pete added, "No better time than now, as you may be making changes to some of the financial reporting and accounts."

Dave could see where this was going. He shook his head and said to Margaret, "Well, what do you think?"

Margaret said, "Dorothy's been telling me Pete needs to retire fully, but I didn't think it would be for a while. But I agree, if we are going to make changes anyway, a good time to make them be when we're getting a new accountant."

I looked at Dave and you could see what he was thinking. I am sure the words, "This has to be Margaret's plan," were ringing in his ears.

"Well, I said, "that's something that we can plan for in the weeks to come. Here's something else: Margaret how much of your time is spent weekly related to financials?"

She answered "Really most of it. Invoicing, paying bills, collection — which takes a lot of my time —, getting stuff ready for the payroll company, doing quarterly taxes. You want me to go on?"

I said, "No, I figured that."

"The problem is nobody else here knows how to do any of the stuff I do."

Then I asked, "Could you tell me on the average how many hours a week you work?"

I could see a light come on in her eyes and she said, "Well, I'm usually the first person here, unless one of the supes comes in to pick up paperwork. I usually close, but Dave — a lot of the time Dave is still here when I leave."

I said, "So, what, ten hours a day?"

She seemed to do some mental calculating and said, "At least. I would say at least ten hours for sure."

I thought for a moment and said, "That can be stressful I bet."

She said, "Well, I don't mind the hours much, as long as everybody does their job right and I don't have to follow behind them and fix their mistakes."

"What kind of mistakes?"

"Oh, you know. A lot of paperwork has to be done right for us to invoice the customers. People pick up things without turning in receipts, and then I get the invoice from the vendors and have nothing to check it against. Stuff like that. I could go on, but we'd be here for awhile."

I said, "I get the picture. But Margaret, even the hours are too long. What about your family life?"

She said, "At home, it's just me and my dogs. As long as I make it to church on Sundays and Wednesday nights, I'm okay."

Pete said, "We have family in Ohio, and when Dorothy and I go there, they ask why Margaret isn't coming."

I looked at Margaret. "I bet you miss them."

"Yes, but someone has to be here."

Dave said, "Margaret, you know I've asked you many times to take time off, and except the Christmas before last, you never would."

I added, "We are going to work on many of the procedures, to make sure the paperwork flows well. But the hours that you put in, and the amount of work you do, are a lot for one person. Don't you agree?"

She smiled and said, "Oh yeah. Dave's been very kind to me, but he gets his money's worth."

Dave, sitting next to Margaret, patted her on the back.

I leaned forward and said, "Margaret, I am going to ask you one thing and I want you to be honest with me, okay?" She nodded once.

"Do you see that this is a problem, not only for you, but even — and maybe mostly — for the company?"

Dave did the best thing he could have done; he looked in her eyes and said, "Margaret, I want you to have time to do your work here, but also time to enjoy it, and not to stress yourself over it."

Margaret said, "I know, and I appreciate that."

That is when I said, "So what do you think we can do to help this situation, besides getting everybody to do their jobs right?"

Margaret thought for few seconds and said, "I guess if we could afford it, we could get some help, someone who could take on some of the work I'm doing now."

This was the moment and the statement I was waiting for. Margaret had (1) accepted that there was a problem, and (2) become willing to ask for help. The rest would be easy. Getting Margaret to give up control would require some strategy as well as tactics, but the first battle had been won. I tried not to look as relieved as I felt.

"Okay, then — let's worry about affordability later. Yes, we need to be able to, but I'm sure we can work that out. Meanwhile, here's what I'd like you to do."

I stood up and drew a rough list with the dry-erase marker on the whiteboard.

List Of Tasks	When it needs to be done	Can someone be trained to do them?	Name anyone in the company who could possibly be able to that job
Task 1	Daily	Yes	Name 1
Task 2	Weekly	No	Name 2
Task 3	Monthly	Yes	No one
Task 4	Quarterly	No	Etc.
Task 5	Annually		

"I want you to make a complete list of all the tasks that you perform," I explained. "And next to each, fill in the other three columns. The only thing I ask you is that for the last two columns, try to be objective, realistic, and honest with yourself. Can you do that?"

I added, "I want to make sure you understand one thing: all the tasks you put down are going to continue to be your responsibility." I grinned and said, "You're not getting off the hook here. I just want to know which jobs lend themselves to being done by someone else. In other words, which ones you can train someone to help you with."

Dave looked as if a light bulb had gone on in his head. He had realized what had just happened. Margaret was going to create this plan and more importantly, she was going to implement it.

I spent the next few minutes explaining the concept of good financial reporting and how these reports would help not just Dave, but everyone, to become more aware of their work, their work efficiency, and most of all, their expense control. Pete participated in the discussion and as an accountant, emphasized several of the points I was making.

Margaret, too, became more engaged and kept telling Dave, "Once we get these changes going, you know you're going to have to have a talk with some of the guys."

Dave commented several times that he knew he had to be more involved than he had been. At one point, he turned to Margaret and said, "You have been telling me these things, I know, but you were right, we needed a coach to make it happen. Now we're moving, and I will get you the help you need."

I ended the session by saying "Okay, guys this is going to take some time, and we have to do it right, but I'm sure now that we're all singing from the same sheet of music. We will create an action plan to make it happen."

I shook Pete's hand and said, "The sooner you get us that accountant, the sooner we can start this process."

"I already have some ideas," he said.

For the next several weeks, we spent most of our time creating an action plan. I must say we had our sticky moments. There was times Margaret had to be coached and reminded of the conference room discussion. Even though it was hard for her to open up her information bank and teach and train others, at the end she did.

During this process we found out one of the part-time project managers, Leo, had accounting experience and wanted more hours. He ended up taking over a lot of the tasks that Margaret was doing. He actually took over all the billing and invoicing.

We started working with a new accounting firm, rather than an individual.

The firm took on a good portion of the training for Leo and Margaret, and within two months I was able to sit with Dave and go over his new P&L and Balance Sheet, showing him areas, he needed to keep an eye on, and even making some changes to turn the bottom line around.

Dave was able to cut his hours and spend more time with Fay and Megan at home.

I received a note from Fay one day that said, "Farid, I have seen Dave more in the last three months then I have seen him in the last three years!"

Also, due to some of our marketing strategies, Dave's company generated over $8 million the following year, and had a net profit of $1.2 million.

This scenario, of one team member, especially an office manager, having full control of the finances of a company, and the owner's not being much involved, is classic in family-owned businesses. It is a risk that most business owners take.

In this particular case we were able to remedy the situation. Margaret came through, and everything worked out. But in at least two other situations, it did not.

I can tell you that in both those cases the office managers had to leave. One quit, and the other had to be terminated.

Again, it is all about every team member being on the bus, heading in the same direction, and most importantly, sitting in the right seat. Sometimes when you ask someone to change seats, they are unhappy – unhappy enough either to get off the bus, or to have to be asked to leave.

WHEN MONEY MATTERS ARE OVERKILL

As important as it is for every business owner to have full control of his or her finances, there are also times when too much emphasis given to every little detail can take your eye off the ball.

I have had clients at one extreme (the majority, by the way), running their business from their checkbook. And then I have had clients who created incredible numbers of different reports, analyzing every aspect of the business: purchases from every vendor, spillage, hourly pay versus salary versus commission, rent versus lease, and so on. They were spending so much of their time analyzing all these reports and charts that they had almost forgotten that they were in business to make money rather than to analyze how it was made. It is what sometimes we refer to as, "analysis paralysis."

There has to be balance in every aspect of the business and money matters are no different. My experience has been that business owners who come from accounting backgrounds are in their comfort zone with numbers. Sometimes they create financials systems and processes that are overkill. Since marketing and sales, or even distribution and delivery, are outside their comfort zone, they spend most of their time analyzing where the money is coming from and where it is going.

On the other hand, business owners like Dave, whose comfort zone is delivery and design, sometimes abdicate their financial responsibilities.

Information is power but it has to be used right. My goal in coaching all my clients has always been to make sure they had the right information, but also used it the right way. The proper use of any information is to help one make the right decision. Too much information can be as bad as no information.

Baroness Susan Greenfield, professor at Oxford said it best *"One has to draw the distinction between knowledge and information. We are in a time when people can sit in front of the screen and get bombarded with facts, and sometimes that's confused for education.*

But I think that what we owe it to our young people to do is to help them ask questions."

Ralph Catts, a University of New England researcher said, *"We need to learn more about how people learn to use information in an effective and efficient manner. Information is all about us but to use it effectively we need skills, not just to find it but to evaluate it."*

Summary

I could have written dozens of other stories related to money matters, but I selected these primarily because through these I hope to convey the main points I wanted the readers to get out of these stories.

1. Make sure you create a financial system that provides you with the right information to make the right decisions.

2. Money matters to all the partners not just the main partner.

3. If you must borrow to finance your business venture, borrowing from your family should be your last resort.

4. If you must borrow from family treat the transaction as if it is same as borrowing from a lending institution or a non-family member

5. Never allow a single person on your team to have more control of your finances than you or other partners.

6. Share your financial goals with your team; after all it is part of their goal to help you achieve them.

7. Do not mix personal expenses with business expenses.

8. Make sure *Trust* is a fundamental part of your business.

9. Make sure you and your team are open to change.

IN CLOSING

It doesn't matter what size business you have, what type of business you are in and who you are in business with. One thing I have learned and witnessed is that every business owner or owners even team members or what people refer to as employees need help and most of all guidance from time to time to be successful and be able to manage every aspect of the business.

Look at business like a competitive game, I let you pick the game, football, basketball, baseball, Olympic games, etc. After all most businesses have competition. A factor that makes one team stronger than the other is their Coach. It is the coach that trains them, guides them but most of all holds them accountable every step of the way.

If you are in business find a good business coach. There are a lot of great business coaches and also business coaching organizations worldwide you can work with.

REFERENCES:

1. QuickBooks ® is an accounting software trademark of Intuit.

2. Peachtree ® is an accounting software trademark of Sage Software.